HURLED INTO GETTYSBURG

POEM STORIES INSPIRED BY THE 1863 BATTLE

6/6/18

To Gary,
Your support means
so much to me...
You are an inspiration...
Thank you!
Theresa

HURLED INTO GETTYSBURG

POEM STORIES INSPIRED BY THE 1863 BATTLE

THERESA WYATT

BLAZEVOX[BOOKS]
Buffalo, New York

Hurled Into Gettysburg
by Theresa Wyatt

Published by BlazeVOX [books]

Printed in the United States of America

Interior design and typesetting by Geoffrey Gatza
Cover Art: Gateway of cemetery, Gettysburg / negative by T.H. O'Sullivan; positive by A Gardner. Library of Congress Prints and Photographs Division Washington, D.C. 20540 USA

First Edition
ISBN: 978-1-60964-303-4
Library of Congress Control Number: 2017954588

BlazeVOX [books]
131 Euclid Ave
Kenmore, NY 14217
Editor@blazevox.org

publisher of weird little books

BlazeVOX [books]

blazevox.org

21 20 19 18 17 16 15 14 13 12 01 02 03 04 05 06 07 08 09 10

BlazeVOX

ACKNOWLEDGMENTS

Grateful acknowledgment is made to the editors of the following publications where these poems first appeared, sometimes in earlier versions.

Prime Number Magazine: ‘Melting” as ‘Gettysburg, July, 1863”
Spillway: “Onions”
The Buffalo News: ‘Hurled Into Gettysburg,” “John Greenleaf Whittier”

The poem, “Melting,” nominated by *Prime Number Magazine*, was named a finalist in *The Best Small Fictions 2017* anthology.

“At the Jennie Wade Monument” and “Hurled Into” previously appeared in the author’s first chapbook *Arrowheads Everywhere,* A Derby by the Lake Project, 2014.

“Trostle Farm at Plum Run,” first published by Seth Jani, *Seven Circle Press,* was reprinted by editors R.D. Pohl (*The Buffalo News*) and Patricia Tansey (*A Celebration of Western New York Poets*). This poem, combined with their kind support, was the initial catalyst for this project. I thank them enormously and find it appropriate to end the book where I began.

Special thanks to Irene Sipos and Peter Siedlecki for their gracious review of this work. Gratitude to Jim Bisco, Rich Olson, Sara Ries, Verneice Turner and good friends all who motivated me with their steadfast encouragement, and to Bill, my husband and road-trip partner through Pennsylvania. And lastly, many thanks to Geoffrey Gatza for supporting this collection.

In Memory Of My Parents
Marietta and Francis Vecere

PREFACE

~ In Honor of the 155th Anniversary of the Battle of Gettysburg ~ 1863 ~ 2018

The Battle of Gettysburg took place over the first three days in July of 1863. The famous battle, which was fought in and around the picturesque Pennsylvania town, is often referenced as "the turning point" in the American Civil War.

The military powers of two armies, the Union's *Army of the Potomac* and the Confederacy's *Army of Northern Virginia*, brought to bear upon the area, an estimated, combined force of over 163,000 men. Casualties from both sides are often cited as over 51,000 – representing those killed, wounded, captured or missing – a horrifying number by any measure.

Through devastating carnage and the aftermath, the Union's victory at Gettysburg became a prescient symbol for a nation that was enduring a great test. For the town's shocked and battle-weary residents, Lincoln's *Gettysburg Address,* delivered but a few months later in November, put their town on the map forever and stirred a nation's conscience.

I'm neither a journalist nor historian. I can't really say exactly why or how the lives of Gettysburg's soldiers and townspeople grabbed me by the shoulders when I first visited there. Simply being awed by what the human spirit survived and how so many acts of human decency and kindness took place after such a bloodbath, has inspired me in ways I cannot fully express.

I look to this history often, gaining fresh optimism and a deeper sense of country every time that I do. It's my hope that maybe even one of these poems might provide similar inspiration, enough to begin or affirm someone else's journey through Gettysburg's remarkable story.

HURLED INTO GETTYSBURG

THE CIVIL WAR

was the great war
of verticality.

The entire march continuously eyed
the top rung, step by step.

The group at the bottom climbed their way up
to Gettysburg, packed heavy aspirations
to last three days.

Were sent back
down the ladder.

The great war of verticality,
of longitude and longing
to be over, was not over

in 1863, rather,

more river and basin washings
were yet to come, more steps to pound,
and oh, think of those steps,

already worn boot smooth,
already thin as beef tea.

VISITING GETTYSBURG

Almost every book begins with mapping the ten roads.
Mentions how like the spokes of a wagon wheel it was,
how the image perfectly fits a carriage-making town.

So I rest here on the Baltimore Pike or the Chambersburg,
then drive up York or west toward Fairfield Road
and it doesn't really matter what road I'm on

or why I can't explain a throbbing heart, bareback,
trying to take it all in as if I knew anything at all
about horses, cannons or bloodshed.

But here I am, parked outside the Cemetery at Evergreen,
with a tightness in my chest that feels oddly strange – as if
the much debated apparitions have slid between my ribs,
are squeezing hard the muscles near my heart, x-raying

my soft spots, sizing me up, grinning wide and placing
heaven bets about how long I'll stay – brainwaves
jumping over snake rail fence.

ELIZABETH C. THORN (1832–1907)

At the Gettysburg Women's Civil War Memorial
Evergreen Cemetery

With a pick axe and spade she dug through
the diabase sill and shale that covered the floor
of the Cemetery Ridge expanse.

These were her war dead now – piled across
her adopted land, limbs reaching the windows
of the arched brick Gatehouse that stood
pummeled like a Roman ruin.

She was all things to all people during those days –
a pregnant mother scout, a stand-in keeper
and grave digger who earned twelve dollars a month,
who later named her daughter Rose Meade
the same November Lincoln spoke.

Some folks may have called her
Beth or Betsy, maybe even Liz
or Lizzie, but to me she's...
Mrs. Thorn...

Gatekeeper of Evergreen Cemetery
from 1862–1865 while her husband
was gone with the Union –

hand to her brow, apron tied,
stones in her shoes – a country
on new footing under her feet.

AT THE JENNIE WADE MONUMENT

Evergreen Cemetery

You lost me, John Burns, when you
tried to sully young Jennie, called her
a she rebel when interviewed.

Some people like their heroes loud
and let them talk, but sometimes history
picks off the scabs of arrogance
when setting records straight.

Seems as though few believed you,
thousands still visit her grave, our flag,
a woman's shawl, warms this site golden.

As for you, the odor you breathed
upon this woman's reputation
blew back on all your glory.

Hero you surely were, John Burns,
and brave – there's no denying –
we see your statue on the battlefield,
your photo in the new museum

where you sit by yourself in a rocking chair,
rifle and crutches close by, a cantankerous
vision in black and white.

SHE

belonged to a secret sewing circle,
hung out quilts on special nights,
sent her daughter to a safe-house
that turned out not to be safe.

She learned the art of abandonment
in the middle of the night because
she was a Negro.

She bargained with the enemy, found
coffee and meat for an angry Colonel
who promised not to take her son.

She watched them guzzle
liquor strength.

She did not stop when they shouted,
Halt or be shot!

She stopped when they shouted,
Halt or be shot!

She carried water until the pump broke,
hauled planks to lay across church pews,
nursed the wounded in her own home,
sold horse bones by the pound for pennies.

Sometimes,
she fell in love.

THE SEMINARY RIDGE MUSEUM

A polite young man at the register
handed me my ticket.

It's extra to go upstairs to the cupola –
that cupola made this town.

And instantly, I'm time-traveled to the scene
where Sam Elliott – playing General Buford –
raises his binoculars, sharpens the lens' focus
and streams *future* into his tactical mind, a mind
that typhoid fever would vanquish in five months.

But on that day, it's easy to imagine the General
descending these stairs in flawless summer light,
uplifted by a cyclorama of clear view, fortified,
ready to make a difference…

I muse over sightlines and pastoral landscapes
all morning long, think about this point in the war,
walk the institution's spiritual halls that once
hosted guarded debate – where discernment

in matters of country and heart meant different things
to different people, especially Seminary students
enrolled from the south who would remember
Buford's name forever.

JOHN GREENLEAF WHITTIER

Founding Member of the American
Anti-Slavery Society, 1833

If you grow up on a farm
in rural Massachusetts and your father
tells you to go out and pick
ripe strawberries

and you come back with pails full
of white ones – so many your parents
and country doctor finally deduce
colorblindness,

I would suspect great compassion
from the mother and father
was sorely needed as the farm
was barely making it.

This listing at Wikipedia:
Great American / Quaker
Abolitionist / Poet and Writer

Colorblindness, not at all useful on a farm,
made choosing just the right flower
and sorting beans a chore,

but useful for a history
stacked with buckets full of gangrene –
a country's highest price – proving itself
worthy of making it see.

THE BEFORE
A New World For Many

Emerald pastures with fragrant mist
over prosperous orchards, a dappled pony
out in the barn with its nose in the hay,

a husband hitching his wagon to go
into town, a wife gazing out the window
through the chores of her everyday.

We came from Germany, they said.
We came from Ireland, Scotland, other places too.
We moved up free from Maryland to settle here,

start over –

ride into town on Sundays, go to our own church,
stop at the confectioner's if he's open 'round back,
window shop before the crops come in.

THE SLAVE HUNTER'S LANTERN

The Other Before

White rays flickered through pines,
if there was moonlight
the coupling could easily be viewed
as something beautiful.

But there was nothing beautiful
about the human hunter's contorted face,
his continuously raised arm.

In the deep woods
with hound dogs running savage,
the slave chaser digging metal spurs
into his horse drawing blood –

light from the lantern exposed all –
the bulging eyes of the horse and dogs,
the dark dark soul of the bounty man

and there was nothing
the illuminating moon
could do, no divinity
anywhere.

WAIT HERE

The Underground Railroad
Adams County & Butler Township

Story goes that Basil Biggs, a well-respected
black man, told his mother he'd make his way
with his hands. He moved cargo in the middle
of the night, went east with his wagon to Yellow Hill
stations in the Quaker Valley where someone from
the Mathews or Griest family would then take over.

Meanwhile, if a starry night was near perfect,
Mag Palm, a laundress and conductress who lived
down Long Lane might be on duty, straddling fences,
listening for muted steps.

In secret, providence holding, decisions pending –
it was all about direction. Coming from McAllister's Mill
near Rock Creek or leaving Yellow Hill – the home
of Phebe Wright in York Springs might prove a good

next leg. Or it could be on to Harrisburg, Philadelphia
or maybe further north to Lewiston where crossing
the cool Niagara was once considered pure delusion.

But first, spent of all energy, they slept on their options –
slept below the cog pit wheel at the Mill, in the old
Native Wind Caves or behind hidden walls, praying

to be clear headed by morning – divinity squeezing
into dark tight spaces, unadorned, invisible.
The next day, light.

PRELUDE

June Double-Quick

A month of worry hearing they were coming – a rush
to send prime stock to Harrisburg. If black, hurry.
Leave your horse with a friend, lie low in the fields,
an ear could be lost to a thrashing sword.

Bury liquor underneath the melon patch, in corn cribs,
under hay-covered slats in the barn, scrape lint, ready
linens and petticoats for bandages.

Secure and bring stores to your cellars, hide Negro friends
in the attic, in the springhouse, get rid of the ladder,
destroy this, cover that, tell no one anything.

Anxiety is up on the roof watching and hearing
the crushing approach of double-quicking soldiers
through the streets. Too many men are out of town.

Oh Lord, where are our boys! someone cries.
The Rebs – They're Here! screams and echoes
through the square.

Practiced, one mother directs,
Take the baby and go to the cellar.
In less than a minute a dozen people follow.

Nineteen women and children, two dogs and a cat
hide in a bank vault on East York Street. This,
or something very much like this, repeats
all over town.

THE TOWN WAS TAKEN OVER

Inspired by the personal reminiscence
of Nellie E. Aughinbaugh at Gettysburg

At times a young woman of nineteen
could be nudged into small talk, even song,
by a flirtatious *Louisiana Tiger* if he was
very winning in his manners.

But when it came to singing
certain patriotic songs with her friends,
Nellie refused these soldiers' requests,
no matter how charmingly solicited

for they had experienced first hand
the fearsome vibrations from
their Rebel Raids in June,

heard too many rumors
to have any change
of heart

and yes, they did speak politely,
maybe even smiled, all the while
waiting for *their* boys

to charge like knights,
and when Buford's men rode in,
they sang with abandon.

JACOB AND SARAH WEIKERT

Taneytown Road Farmhouse

It is fair and just to call a man
who lived near Little Round Top
a good man, a good husband

who ran back in the house
for his wife's new petticoat
after she insisted.

She, having borne thirteen children,
giving no mind to the panic
or foreseen misery in the air
she breathed,

not ever knowing before
the sort of misery she was
about to witness,

but having a mind
perhaps, of candid,
loving expectation.

A TEENAGE PERSPECTIVE

All of her senses were fifteen years old.
Fear that caused trembling was a new
gripping menace rising inside her.

From a window in the barn she saw
a sergeant beat a soldier down when he
cried out for water, weak from everything.

One ghoulish scene followed another,
engraving her memory, scratching deep,

and she was filled with biting shame

thinking of her brother whom she scolded
the night before he enlisted
for eating her pie.

But today, hot tears run down
a petrified face, sunlight bouncing
off sabers by thousands, dazzling
in their snaking swirls of clarity.

UNINVITED GUESTS

Some soldiers ran away from blurry waves
of marching lines through the countryside

and blustered their way into kitchens
and sheds much uninvited.

The town women, many alone and alert
on all fronts, called these men skedaddlers.

Be it known these women gave as good as they got,
a young girl recalls her mother saying,

If you put but one finger in my apple butter crocks,
you had better plan to sleep standing up
all night long with your eyes open!
Or else, you can ask me proper.

HURLED INTO GETTYSBURG

What sort of soldiers were they, wolfing
baking soda – ripping heads and tail off
mackerel with no pause, animal like –
by history's telling of the hunger.

Who ransacked pregnant women's houses,
soiled their flour and yeast, blew out
their barns and windows for more
excruciating clarity.

Who left behind the flood of amputation,
red gullies on linens, dumped limbs inside
featherbed quilts, but not before taking the china.

Mothers of war have told us what sort
of bootless men and boys they were:
Every lice infested starving soldier
is someone else's son, they said.

Someone else's son hurled viciously
into other worlds barefoot, war's special
Sundays of cannonball choruses,

crying voices

absorbed into the night sound
of crickets that won't
let you sleep.

ONIONS

Try to understand the ailment,
the mental anguish flare-ups –
It's not fair, if only I was born…

and at every dawn's rise to know
you're indispensable yet disposable,
smoky hills offering no clearing
in the dividing landscape.

Who would they blame
for this duality that sliced sleep,
opened blisters on their feet,
blasted every simple thing.

Consider then, the possible
throbbing questions, unanswerable
inside military clay mouths.

Will the onions be sweet tonight
when we bite into them?

Their only ration for the day – rivulets
of juice trickling down gun powder chins,
skin cracked like shrunken earth
after an epic drought.

A CHERRY TREE

Partially Based on Confederate
Pvt. Benjamin Thorp's Account

There was a log with notches
carved into it, ladder like,
resting up against a cherry tree
in an open field,

set there for harvest season
and other sweet summer days.

With twenty-twenty vision, a fast
and furious Reb footed his way up
with sharpshooter precision
and picked off General Reynolds.

Word spread throughout divisions, men wept,
peaceful orchards earthquake rumbled – released
their injured fruit – Willoughby Run streamed red.

It was just the beginning for this vast relic park –
parrott balls crashed into trunks, too many
witness trees to count.

JOHNNY REB & BILLY YANK

About Brothers John Wesley & William E. Culp

Hope for both of them, one in dark blue wool,
the other in butternut, was to win the next battle
and when finally over, prop a haversack under
their heads at night containing their present lives:
hard tack, tin cups and pictures of their ladies.

Both propped below stars – turncoat stars
that coarsely covered each of them then,
smothering boyhood memories of lying
on their backs in summer with silky grass
between their ears – morphing stars

that gathered in brigades of grisly orbs
above Devil's Den, McPherson Ridge,
Culp's Hill – and by the blue canopy of day,
no one tracing animal shapes in clouds.

And at home, one family between them, looking up
at the same sky, knowing all heads were propped,
each thinking of the other, wondering
if tomorrow would be the day.

MELTING

One soldier took a bullet
which shattered his femur.

The next day he woke up
in a cellar with a woman
leaning over him

picking wax
from his beard.

She apologized, said the doctor
needed light to operate in the dark.

Candles melted down to nothing
were stuck everywhere – even
in her bonnet.

GRATITUDE

I wish to make a correction to
my statement that all was lost.
~ Lydia Ziegler Clare

Imagine yourself
at age thirteen
returning home
after battle flight
seeing just the feet
of your family's hogs
lying in the pen, but
overjoyed at finding your
two beautiful white cows
still alive – hefty animals
standing unfazed
after storied crossfire,
divine four-legged
angel mothers
mustered in
ready for duty
milk at hand.

PEPPERMINT

Perpendicular to some unknown heaven
were bones rising and jutting out
in all directions.

Covering her nose with a handkerchief dipped
in peppermint, she had to step over darkening bodies,
her shoes sinking into filthy sucking mud for it rained hard
the day they came up from the cellars.

And surely, because she was shaken, thinking about
her fiancé, whereabouts unknown, when she saw
a clutched medal or photo rouged in blood near
one of the bodies, she broke down – crazed

by riddled memory – for this was the same road
they strolled in May, his warm palm in hers,
apple blossoms bursting forth…but

this morning – the idea of *forever* now – is
a charred canvas edging a girl zigzagging home,
giving cover to jack rabbits darting about,
trying not to step on live shells.

JENNIE & JACK

Mary Virginia Wade (5/21/1843 - 7/3/1863)
Cpl. Johnston H. Skelly, Jr. (8/4/1841 - 7/12/1863)

My Dearest Jack…do try and get a furlough. It is one year
since I seen you…Always your true friend and well wisher.
Jennie M. Wade…I send my love…January 24th, 1863

They died nine days apart – neither knowing about
the other – she with a bullet lodged in her corset, a photo
of him in her apron pocket, dough on her fingers,
her sister's infant baby just feet away.

The only civilian to die by a sniper's bullet – soldiers
from New York dug her grave, remembered her duty
and kindness, paid their respects – for she never took
a penny for the bread she gave them.

He died from likely indifference – an arm wound
that festered for nearly a month, a captured Corporal
at the *Battle at Carter's Woods* – covered in neglect,
fever of coldness – talk of a drunken surgeon.

Dear Mother, I received your ever welcome letter…This is the
prettiest village I have ever seen since I am in Virginia…Did
you get the money we sent from Clarksburg…Nothing more
at present, but remain your affectionate son. Johnston H. Skelly

Who doesn't love a love story – can't picture this childhood
duo of friendship coming of age, plotting their futures
on a sleigh ride up and down the Baltimore Pike – passing
Evergreen Cemetery under a blanket of soft winter white.

Dearest Jack…it is snowing very fast here. The snow
is about six inches deep. If it keeps on for a few hours
we will have sleighing…February 22nd, 1863

DAY THREE

87 Degrees

Leaders from both sides hailed from West Point
with various standing in their graduating classes.
Later, much would be made of this, analyzed,
mulled over at campfires and shot up taverns.

After *Pickett's Charge*, the what-nots and where-fores
in regard to military training were parsed for publication.
At times, the discourse surrounding obedience and direct
orders took center stage, often by those who were never
center stage.

Those left standing kissed victory in their minds as if
victory was a woman and they were on their way home.
Ominous hunches fell upon the others concerning
the coming fall and winter – all quite possible
since nothing was resolved for certain. Crazy,
thoughts of cold and pure white snow
on a day like that.

ABOUT SALLIE CORBELL PICKETT (1843-1931)

Wife of Confederate General George E. Pickett

"Before the war, they were happy," he said, quoting our textbook."
~ Natasha Trethewey, from "Southern History," *Native Guard*

After bearing colossal humiliations from the notorious
lost battle where no Hercules or Trojan Horse advanced
their ultimate cause – what man would not desire a wife
to later lionize him?

She was perfect for *her soldier* – a literary talent skilled
in myth, a widow with needs to revise, romanticize, enable
a reputation that would stick like honey on tall statues
and twisted reconciliations.

Inventing courage with a new math of words, she added
and subtracted, for she loved him like opportunity – and
her books flowed forth like rivers rising during floods,
murky currents steering the peculiar

Lost Cause Literature

where post-war southern conscience infused itself
with happy faces of former slaves and just enough scent
from sweet magnolias as to blush and be noticed.

RECONSTRUCTING

To all the gods –
my queries remain fixed
rising from a doubting youth,

unanswerable I know
inside the land of cotton mouths
and lurid cross burnings.

But why did you run away?
What did you use to cover your ears
and shield your eyes when bullets

scored and paralyzed
your church bells soundless,
made deaf your faithful brethren?

DEAD LETTER OFFICE
Time Travel Division / Gettysburg Post Office

Dear Mrs. Georgia Wade McClellan,
Thank you for the clock that your family donated to
your sister's museum house. It's still set at eight-thirty.

Dear Mr. Randolph Johnston,
You, Lloyd Watts, and many others are owed reparations.
Having served honorably in the 24th US Colored Infantry,
you came home to segregated cemeteries and parades.
How did you muster the fortitude to organize *The Sons
of Good Will,* sustain belief that all men are created equal?

Dear Annie Etheridge, Nurse, 3rd Michigan,
The photo of you wearing the distinguished *Kearny Cross*
in honor of your courage is not one I will soon forget.

Dear Mrs. Elmina Spencer, Matron of the 147th New York,
As an accomplished equestrian, riding up to forty miles a day
bringing supplies to hospital camps, did you meet General Grant
when he issued your special permit to pass through Union lines?
Oswego, New York must be very proud of you. I'm sorry it took
so long for your pension to be increased.

Dear Mrs. Catherine Trostle,
It was disturbing to learn that your claim for devastating
damages to your property was denied. The photo of your barn
with all the dead horses lying in front is famous. Millions of people
have visited your family's home since your heirs sold
your land to the National Park Service in 1899.

Thank you.

VISIONS

On great fields something stays. Forms change and pass;
bodies disappear, but spirits linger, to consecrate ground
for the vision place of souls. ~ Col. Joshua L. Chamberlain

When I climbed Little Round Top and stood there still,
they came to me. My mind spliced old films together.
I imagined breezes floating bible pages away, saw them
feather down hills toward field hospitals a few miles out,

white tents set up by the hundreds – row upon row,
wing-like, shrouding what was to come in a few days' time
when the trains blew in – when the lucky, able to be moved,
heard whistles through delirium calling their names.

And they were hoisted up on stretchers above the rails
leaving the vision place behind, their phantom limbs
weightless.

CAMP LETTERMAN

Why the rough edge of beauty?
~ Natasha Trethewey, *Native Guard*

My hotel on York Road stands on what was once
Camp Letterman, a new style field hospital that utilized
triage and tent stations, including embalming, and became
a model in the aftermath. Further back is *Giant Supermarket*
and just across the way there's a *Perkin's Restaurant* where
the pleasant smell of morning coffee and bacon permeates
the air. In my direct view are railroad tracks, tree clusters
not far beyond the commerce and like so many
of my days here, brilliant recurring visions.

This time I see nurses descending train steps – carrying
satchels and bundles of lavender sachets, eyes wincing
from the assault of scorched hair and indescribable stench.
They move swiftly toward camp, toward daily courses
of cauldron boiling, dipping and pouring.
Above some tents, I picture the beautiful wreaths
from the park ranger's photos – cedar, pine, eucalyptus –
all tasked with keeping insects and vermin away,

not dipped in gold like Roman wreaths,
not properly shaped like the Greeks' *laurel nobilis*
nor Apollo's crown, but humble rustic wreaths –
boughs and garlands of brutal victory, fashioned
with teary eyes, festooning the purest grief.

And mercifully, as was thought by poets, away from
manic telegraph lines, nature sent condolences to comfort
them all – the wide embrace of tree shade, gentle breezes,
the music of rippling water through streams nearby.

A REFLECTION
Reading Monuments

Rain and drizzle creates a soft misty veil
on the monuments – droplets catch inside crevices
of dynamic men, in beards that held grief
and strong jaws that labored not to look afraid.

Here I see my father, my brother, my husband,
your father, your brother, your husband and son
like all sons – raised up not to cry or show fear,
jaws still set working against any sign

of weakness, eyes born trained
in chronic mode of surveillance,
protecting us yet.

REQUIEM

Branches unbraid, invert
themselves in the reclamation
of ancestry.

Time travels to another family tree
retired, emptied from its universe
of work and war.

In fall, muted yellow shrouds this mausoleum,
limbs lower tactically to examine remains,
evaluate the mites of decay, mingle with
the essence of gently sifted soils.

All around us – the sound
of quiet requiem honors all –
seeps through windows and veins
of desiccated leaves, lands on dust.

Egress through monuments, warm yellow
auburn and sage – an illumination of sorts –
I see voyeur roots peer through openings
marking their time toward spring

when new hymns will shoot from branches,
when the DNA of patience and history

will breathe into the wind –
So much green yet to come.

TROSTLE FARM AT PLUM RUN

The breastworks seemed
to whisper

go lie in this open field
and feel the earth
speak to you,

allow the ground
to tell you its story,
how stampedes and strife
were often daily

and how,
the in between times
accommodated lovers
at the beginning of their thirst.

Allow yourself
the curiosity of tall tales
and sad but true testimony
of how this battle
or that battle
changed the course
of history,

and how
as you see it
lying there in an open field,

how drops of ruby blood
invisible to sight or touch
have mingled into blooms.

REFERENCES / BIBLIOGRAPHY

Creighton, Margaret S. *The Colors of Courage, Gettysburg's Forgotten History*, Basic Books, Perseus Books Group, New York, 2005

Conklin, Eileen F. *Women at Gettysburg 1863*, Gettysburg, PA, Thomas Publications, 1993

Small, Cindy L. *The Jennie Wade Story: A True and Complete Account of the Only Civilian Killed During the Battle of Gettysburg.* Gettysburg, PA, Thomas Publications, 1991

CREDIT NOTES ON SPECIFIC POEMS

"A Cherry Tree"
Slade, Jim & John Alexander. *Firestorm at Gettysburg*. Schiffer Publishing, LTD, Atglen, PA, (page 55) Private Benjamin P. Thorp, Confederate sharpshooter, 55th NC Infantry, claims to have shot General Reynolds. Also spelled as "Thorpe" in various citations.

"About Sallie Corbell Pickett"
Gordon, L.J. "*LaSalle Corbell Pickett (1843-1931)*," Encyclopedia Virginia. Virginia Foundation for the Humanities, 27 Oct. 2015. Web. 20 Feb. 2017

"Gratitude"
Clare, Lydia Ziegler & Hugh Ziegler, "*A Gettysburg Girl's Story of the Great Battle*," Adams County Historical Society Archive, Gettysburg, PA (No date)

"Jennie & Jack"
Small, Cindy L. *The Jennie Wade Story*. Gettysburg, PA, Thomas Publications, 1991; D'Alessandro, Enrica. *My Country Needs Me*, "The Story of Corporal Johnston Hastings Skelly, Jr.," Quotations from letters dated 1/24/1863, pages 92-93; from 10/29/1862, pages 63-64; from 2/22/1863, page 94, Schroeder Publications, Lynchburg, VA, 2012

"Prelude"
Slade, Jim & John Alexander, *Firestorm at Gettysburg*, page 61, bank vault reference from the Jennie S. Croll account with added footnote.

"The Town Was Taken Over"
Aughinbaugh, Nellie E. *Personal Experiences of a Young Girl During the Battle of Gettysburg*, Adams County Historical Society, Gettysburg Civilian Accounts Collection, 2014

"Wait Here, The Underground Railroad"
McCauslin, Deborah Sandoe. *Yellow Hill, Reconstructing the Past: Puzzle of a Lost Community*, For the Cause Productions, Gettysburg, PA, 2007

Theresa Wyatt was born and raised in Buffalo, New York. After obtaining her Master's Degree in Art Education, she primarily worked with students-at-risk, her longest tenure with the NYS Department of Corrections. In retirement, she eagerly returned to creative writing. Her poetry has appeared in the *American Journal of Hospice & Palliative Medicine*, *Earth's Daughters*, *Hektoen International Journal*, *Spillway*, *steel bellow*, *The Buffalo News*, *The Healing Muse* and *The Medical Literary Messenger*. She is a recent finalist in the *Prime Number Magazine Award for Poetry 2017* and *The Best Small Fictions 2017*. Her first self-published chapbook titled, *Arrowheads Everywhere*, appeared in 2014. She credits her parents, many excellent teachers and talented friends for her exposure to the arts and for her love of books. The author and her husband reside south of the city in the Town of Evans near Lake Erie.

86055154R00031

Made in the USA
Columbia, SC
07 January 2018